TWEAKING
THE CASE FOR IN
MULTINATIONAL

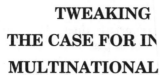

Raymond A. Millen

Books Express

Specialist suppliers of Military History and Defence Studies
P.O. Box 10, Saffron Walden, Essex, CB11 4EW. U.K.
Tel: 01799 513726, Fax: 01799 513248
info@books-express.co.uk / www.books-express.co.uk

June 2002

The author would like to thank Dr. Thomas-Durell Young and Lieutenant Colonel Brian Lovatt (Ret) for insightful comments on earlier drafts of the manuscript. Any errors or misinterpretations which remain do so despite their best efforts.

*****

Comments pertaining to this report are invited and should be forwarded to: Director, Strategic Studies Institute, U.S. Army War College, 122 Forbes Ave., Carlisle, PA 17013-5244. Copies of this report may be obtained from the Publications Office by calling (717) 245-4133, FAX (717) 245-3820, or via the Internet at Rita.Rummel@ carlisle.army.mil

*****

Most 1993, 1994, and all later Strategic Studies Institute (SSI) monographs are available on the SSI Homepage for electronic dissemination. SSI's Homepage address is: http://www.carlisle.army. mil/usassi/welcome.htm

*****

The Strategic Studies Institute publishes a monthly e-mail newsletter to update the national security community on the research of our analysts, recent and forthcoming publications, and upcoming conferences sponsored by the Institute. Each newsletter also provides a strategic commentary by one of our research analysts. If you are interested in receiving this newsletter, please let us know by e-mail at outreach@carlisle.army.mil or by calling (717) 245-3133.

ISBN 1-58487-092-3

FOREWORD

In 1931, General of the Army Douglas MacArthur penned the following thoughts on innovation: "We must hold our minds alert and receptive to the application of unglimpsed methods and weapons. The next war will be won in the future, not in the past. We must go on, or we will go under." As the North Atlantic Treaty Organization (NATO) adapts to the emerging strategic environment, it must consider innovative organizational structures that will allow it to harness the potential of its European partners.

In this monograph, Lieutenant Colonel Raymond Millen examines NATO's enduring deficiencies and their detrimental effect on military capabilities. The decade following the end of the Cold War has revealed a far different world than envisioned. As the United States ruefully discovered, the reduced threat did not diminish security obligations. NATO's European members hoped otherwise and paid insufficient attention to military capabilities. NATO enlargement exacerbates the existing problems. NATO's integrated military structure does not easily accommodate the new members, which still suffer from the effects of the Soviet system. Simply put, their nascent market economies and unsophisticated militaries represent great obstacles to NATO interoperability.

Lieutenant Colonel Millen explores the establishment of integrated multinational divisions as a solution to NATO's salient problems. The co-stationing of Allied units in existing casernes and under a host division headquarters certainly provides opportunities worth discussing. Streamlining the Alliance to a single active corps of ten divisions and the establishment of a robust logistical supply group permits greater utility of limited manpower and equipment. Under this structure, all Alliance members can focus modernization on select units and become active participants in all NATO operations.

As Lieutenant Colonel Millen points out, this bold approach creates challenges for the Alliance, but the tremendous benefits outweigh the short-term risks. To remain relevant, the Alliance must seek innovations. Otherwise, it will become a Cold War relic.

The Strategic Studies Institute is pleased to offer this monograph as a topic of debate that will continue well into the millennium.

DOUGLAS C. LOVELACE, JR.
Director
Strategic Studies Institute

BIOGRAPHICAL SKETCH OF THE AUTHOR

RAYMOND A. MILLEN is currently assigned as the Director of European Security Studies at the Strategic Studies Institute. A lieutenant colonel in the U.S. Army, he graduated from the U.S. Military Academy in 1982, was commissioned as an infantry officer, and has held a variety of command and staff assignments in Germany and Continental United States. He commanded a light infantry company during Operation JUST CAUSE, the invasion of Panama in 1990. Lieutenant Colonel Millen has also served as the U.S. Army Infantry School Liaison Officer to the German Infantry School at Hammelburg, Germany; Battalion Executive Officer, 3-502d Infantry, Fort Campbell, Kentucky; and Chief of Intelligence Section and Balkans Team Chief, Survey Section, SHAPE, Belgium. He is a graduate of the U.S. Army's Command and General Staff College, and holds an M.A. degree in National Security Studies from Georgetown University. He is a Foreign Area Officer for Western Europe. Lieutenant Colonel Millen has published articles in a number of scholarly and professional journals, including *Infantry Magazine* and *The Swiss Military Journal*. His book, *Command Legacy*, was published by Brasseys in April 2002.

SUMMARY

The greatest peril to NATO is not a matter of relevancy but rather the inability to adapt to European realities and enduring deficiencies. Insufficient military spending and investment as well as significant downsizing have resulted in an ever-widening capabilities and interoperability gulf between the United States and the Alliance partners. The Defense Capabilities Initiative will likely not bear fruit because the Allies are incapable of correcting the identified deficiencies under existing budget constraints. NATO may have broadened its mandate to include crisis response operations, but European military forces are incapable of swift power projection and will suffer inveterate manpower shortages for deployed forces. Multinational corps and divisions suffer from the enduring problems with command authority, transfer of authority, and corps combat service support. NATO's approach to multinational formations suffers from a lack of true integration. Subordinate units are isolated from each other until assembled for a crisis. This approach is akin to baking a cake without mixing the ingredients beforehand.

The problems associated with veteran members pale in comparison to NATO's new members and candidates. The lingering effects of the communist economies and the Soviet integrated military structure represent enduring barriers to swift integration with the Alliance. Several more years of reforms are necessary before the new members can contribute to the existing NATO integrated military structure. Financing a modern, interoperable force is simply beyond their economic capabilities. NATO enlargement is a superb initiative, enhancing European stability and security, but without the ability to harness the potential of new members, NATO will lamentably view them as not-ready-for-primetime and continue to marginalize them.

The vast majority of NATO's ailments can be cured by the adoption of integrated multinational divisions (IMD), meaning the subordinate brigades and battalions are stationed together under the host division headquarters. The IMD allows every NATO member to contribute forces according to its size and relative wealth. Integration of new members will proceed more quickly and assuredly because they have the opportunity to train intimately with Allied units. Language immersion as well as daily contact with democratic values and Western culture creates stronger bonds among members. For the Alliance as a whole, IMDs allow for a greater pooling of resources and manpower and permit focused modernization of the force contributions.

IMDs permit NATO to rely on the Allied Command Europe Rapid Reaction Corps (ARRC) as the centerpiece of the Alliance with a dedicated, robust combat service support group and rotating commanding general. Maintenance and modernization of two other corps headquarters are crucial to ensure seamless command and control for enduring peace support operations. Such an approach permits Allies to lower the readiness of their remaining divisions and brigades until mobilized for major threats. The result is a more cohesive, modern, mobile NATO at a pittance of the current cost. Perhaps, these reforms can lower the defense spending obligation to 1.5 percent of the gross domestic product (GDP) without lowering military capabilities.

Recommendations.

The United States can improve its strategic position and cohesion by pursuing the following:

- Convert the two U.S. divisions in Europe into IMDs in order to assist in the assimilation of new members into the Alliance.

- Encourage other NATO members to adopt this model in order to make more effective use of their military spending and resources.

- Establish the ARRC as NATO's higher readiness force for all missions and maintain the EUROCORPS and EUROFOR corps headquarters, sufficiently staffed and equipped with the most modern and robust command and control systems. Rotate the command of the ARRC among the contributing members.

- Expand the existing ARRC combat support (CS) and combat service support (CSS) base into an Area Support Group (ASG) equivalent to provide assured logistics during training and deployments. The ASG must be sufficiently large to support multiple rotations during extended peace support operations (PSO).

The IMD architecture means that all Allies share responsibilities, risks, and benefits. With all members actively engaged in operations, the United States will not feel compelled to take unilateral military action or constantly bear the lion's share of military operations. Making the necessary reforms will be a challenge and will require substantial marketing of the idea, but the alternative solutions are no cure. NATO must break the mold and grasp the opportunities.

TWEAKING NATO:
THE CASE FOR INTEGRATED
MULTINATIONAL DIVISIONS

Introduction.

NATO continues as the most successful and enduring alliance in history. Notwithstanding a handful of dissenting viewpoints, NATO has no security peers. Even so, its preeminent role in European security is not a foregone conclusion. Given Europe's stable situation, NATO's continued relevance is predicated less on collective defense than on collective security.

Post-Cold War initiatives, such as the Defense Capabilities Initiative, Combined Joint Task Force, and the European Security and Defense Policy, are laudable but address the manifestations and not the ailments plaguing the Alliance: burden sharing, command authority, interoperability, and diminishing military capabilities. The current political atmosphere and integrated military structure cannot reconcile these opposing forces. Another approach is needed—integrated multinational divisions (IMDs). At first glance, the reader may dismiss this approach as hackneyed, but the details reveal its practicability.

The first part of this monograph examines the enduring European NATO member deficiencies and the chronic assimilation difficulties of new members with the Alliance. The second part examines the opportunities presented through the restructuring of NATO nation land forces into IMDs and some recommendations for streamlining the integrated military structure. Through such reforms, NATO will gain enhanced interoperability, equalize burden sharing, mitigate ongoing command authority issues and accommodate existing lower defense spending. The U.S. Army will benefit by cultivating the military potential of

1

every member and allowing it to realign forces in accordance with U.S. National Security Strategy and National Military Strategy without commitment penalties. Consequently, NATO not only will continue to be relevant but also a more cohesive and adaptive security organization for the future strategic environment.

European Deficiencies.

Technological Shortcomings. The technological gap between the United States and its NATO Allies is increasing, adversely affecting interoperability and Europe's ability to contribute to NATO combat operations. The origins of this predicament stem from Europe's pursuit of a peace dividend in the post-Cold War period. European force level reductions resulting from the Conventional Forces in Europe treaty and the global recession in the early 1990s prompted governments to divert more funds from defense budgets to domestic spending. In the process, European governments particularly assigned a lower budgetary priority to military research and development, which has shrunk to approximately one-third of the U.S. defense research budget.[1]

Insufficient apportionment of the gross domestic product (GDP) to military spending has led to a significant degradation of European military capabilities (Table 1). NATO has established a goal of 2.0 percent of GDP as the minimum apportionment for defense spending for the purpose of maintaining burden sharing.[2] Unfortunately, half of the NATO members fail to meet the established goal and appear incapable of meeting their obligations.[3] European counterclaims that much money is spent on economic assistance to Eastern European countries and similar activities are red herrings. This diversion of funds may indeed enhance regional stability but does nothing for the health of the Alliance. Financial obligations to the Alliance should remain the dominant focus, but the political will is lacking, particularly when domestic social issues are

2

more pressing. NATO has yet to address the arrears adequately, and the decline in European armed forces continues.

State	Active Force Size. 2000[a]	Defense Expenditures, (FY)[b]	Percent GDP Military Expenditure, (FY)[b]	Defense Expenditure per Troop in US $[c]
Belgium	39,250	$2.5 billion (01)	1.2 (99)	$63,694
Czech Rep.	57,700	$1.2 billion (01)	2.2 (01)	$20,797
Denmark	21,810	$2.5 billion (99)	1.4 (99)	$114,626
France	249,430	$39.8 billion (97)	2.5 (97)	$159,564
Germany	321,300	$32.8 billion (98)	1.5 (98)	$102,085
Greece	159,170	$6.1 billion (99/00)	4.9 (99/00)	$38,324
Hungary	43,790	$822 million (2000)	1.6 (00)	$18,771
Iceland	120[d]	0	0	0
Italy	250,600	$20.7 billion (00/01)	1.7 (00/01)	$82,602
Luxembourg	899	$131 million (98/99)	1.0 (98/99)	$145,717
Netherlands	51,940	$6.5 billion (00/01)	1.5 (00/01)	$125,144
Norway	26,700	$3.1 billion (98)	2.1 (98)	$116,105
Poland	217,290	$3.2 billion (00)	2.0 (00)	$14,727
Portugal	44,650	$2.5 billion (97)	2.6 (97)	$55,991
Spain	166,050	$6 billion (97)	1.1 (97)	$36,134
Turkey	609,700	$10.6 billion (99)	5.6 (99)	$17,386
UK	212,450	$36.9 billion (97)	2.7 (97)	$173,688
USA	1,365,800	$276.7 billion (99)	3.2 (99)	$202,592
Canada	59,100	7.5 billion (00/01)	1.3 (00/01)	$126,904

[a] IISS, *The Military Balance 2000-2001.*
[b] *CIA World Fact Book.*
[c] Derived by dividing Defense Expenditures by Active Force Size.
[d] Paramilitary forces.

Table 1. Defense Expenditures of NATO States.

Defense expenditures per troop indicate the general sophistication of the respective armed forces. Ideally, small, modernized active forces are the most use to the Alliance. The larger the defense expenditure per troop, the more interoperability is enhanced.[4] Most of the bottom half falls well below the average expenditure (excluding Iceland) of $89,714, reflecting the wide disparity of sophistication within the Alliance.

European NATO nations' negligence of the armed forces became apparent during the NATO-led operations in Bosnia (1995) and Kosovo (1999). The United States bore the brunt of the fighting in both air campaigns, flying approximately 70 percent of the all sorties, expending 80 percent of the precision-guided munitions, and providing practically all of the aviation electronic warfare support; both operations revealed the growing technological gap between the United States and the European allies.[5] Specifically, the Kosovo conflict revealed deficiencies in "cruise missiles, radar satellite observation systems, offensive jammers, [and] aircraft identification systems."[6]

European military capabilities have plummeted in other areas as well. Strategic airlift capabilities are far from adequate, and procurement of an intra-theater aircraft is progressing very slowly. Reconnaissance and surveillance platforms are few. Stand-off, precision guided munitions take years to procure in proper amounts and require extensive training of soldiers. Budget constraints have lowered pilot flying hours below the minimum of 120 hours per pilot per year.[7]

Admittedly, the Alliance has taken steps to correct the European deficiencies. The 1999 Washington Summit instituted the Defense Capabilities Initiative (DCI), whose goal was to close the capabilities gap and improve interoperability.[8] With an eye on the future, DCI sought to "improve defense capabilities to ensure the effectiveness of future multinational operations across the full spectrum of Alliance missions . . ."[9] The identified deficiencies were

4

broken down into 59 measures and grouped into 5 discrete areas:

- Deployability and mobility;

- Sustainability and logistics;

- Survivability of forces and infrastructure;

- Effective engagement; and,

- Consultation, Command and Control and Information Systems.[10]

Unfortunately, 50 percent of the measures have proven to be resource intensive and beyond the capabilities of the individual members. Ultimately, any DCI improvement requires cooperative initiatives, such as consortia, research and development sharing, and the leasing or selling of equipment.[11] Given the numerous shortfalls of European armed forces, it is little wonder that some in the United States are reluctant to engage in coalition warfare with the European allies. This is not to say that European NATO nations cannot or will not increase their military technology. Improvements will come, albeit slowly and definitely lagging behind the United States. The technology gap is symptomatic of a European attitude that the United States will provide security assurance no matter how insouciant European concerns. Casting aside all the rhetoric of pan-Europeanists, the future European Union will not likely progress beyond a confederacy of states, and all the security problems associated with confederacies will persist.

Organizational Shortcomings. European land forces are still largely oriented towards territorial defense rather than expeditionary missions. In view of NATO's acceptance of conflict prevention and crisis management tasks to include peace support operations, European participation is hampered by poor power projection capabilities and manpower limitations as a result of conscription.[12]

In the past decade, European NATO countries have downsized their armed forces with insufficient attention to modernization and reform. They have reduced the number of divisions, but the remaining forces are still as heavy as their Cold War predecessors. Transforming land forces into lighter, more agile, and more effective instruments is expensive and time-consuming. Given the current levels of military spending, the transformation of European armies will progress slowly at best. Without strategic airlift or sealift, European power projection capabilities are limited mainly to rail and road transportation. Hence, for the most part, European militaries are not tailored for crisis reaction operations.

The issue of conscription is much more problematic. While some European countries have professional armies, many have retained conscription either wholly or partially because it is the most cost effective way to fill the ranks.[13] Conscript forces are not as capable as professional forces because lower pay and shortened military service obligations (ranging from 8 to 12 months) produce an ill-trained and relatively unmotivated soldier.[14]

Conscription limits the force size a country can deploy to a crisis area. Many countries with conscription cannot legally deploy their conscripts out-of-area. Since conscripts are largely lower-ranking soldiers—the work horses—the officers and noncommissioned officers must take up the slack. Moreover, soldiers in specialty positions (staff, communications, intelligence, and so forth) are in high demand and are deployed much more frequently than planned. To fulfill the manpower requirements of a deploying unit, nondeploying units must contribute personnel and usually key equipment. Experience suggests that peace support operations require the dedication of three units (usually battalions) for each mission requirement—the unit deployed, the unit preparing for the deployment, and the unit recovering from the deployment. Manpower problems multiply whenever a deployment or multiple deployments lasts months, forcing the armed

6

forces to use the same personnel or units more often than foreseen. Trained soldiers leave the service in frustration or exhaustion. To counter this trend, some countries may offer significant pay incentives, but this approach makes extended deployments exorbitantly expensive and devours the military budget.

The average term of European conscript service is 12 months or less. Even if a country permitted the use of conscripts for out-of-area deployments, the deployment window of opportunity is small. The average conscript spends 4-6 months for initial training. Soldiers need at least a month in a unit before they become familiar with procedures. Since most crises rarely fall in sync with the conscription service cycle, the deployment time of each conscript will only be a few months. Without any special crisis provisions in national laws, managing the personnel requirements alone during a crisis can be overwhelming.

Conversion to a professional army has ramifications though. Countries that have converted to a volunteer force without concomitant increases in incentives suffer acute manpower shortages. Without adequate pay, medical and retirement benefits, accommodations, and family incentives among others, few citizens will volunteer to serve their country for a 3-year tour. Investment in the soldier is not the only expense either. Recruitment requires sophisticated marketing initiatives, meaning the government must engage a professional marketing firm to be successful. Demographics for each country are unique. A recruitment campaign for one country may not work in another. For example, the United States promises financial support for college in its recruitment advertisements. Such an approach means little to Europeans since college is almost regarded as a right. It may be that a European will respond to the societal prestige of military service. Regardless, a successful recruitment program requires significant financing.

Because of the need for incentives and the concomitant expenses, the size of European professional armies will be small, perhaps no more than one to two divisions per country. Whether a country relies on conscription or a professional force, the result is fewer forces available for crisis reaction operations.

NATO Structural Shortcomings.

Integrated Military Structure Shortcomings. NATO's integrated military structure still retains much of its Cold War arrangements, making it ill-suited for expeditionary operations and limiting the benefits of enlargement.

Despite the shift towards multinational formations, NATO's basic military building block still rests on national divisions, meaning that each member country contributes divisions to the Alliance for use in traditional Article 5 (collective defense) or non-Article 5 (conflict prevention and crisis management to include peace support operations). This arrangement was practicable during the Cold War since the Alliance's sole focus was on territorial collective defense, and the need for simplicity overrode any initiatives towards greater military efficiency among its members. NATO organized the General Defense Plan of Germany into eight national corps, whose commanders retained crucial command authorities, e.g. authority over training, logistics, task organization, and mission assignments, among others.[15] Theoretically, greater military coordination could be effected among the members upon a war alert since the Alliance could expect a few weeks of preparation time before the Warsaw Pact could generate the needed offensive power for an attack.

With NATO's extension of its mandate to include non-Article 5 missions, these Cold War arrangements required revision. The shift from a territorial orientation to an expeditionary posture has profound implications on the ground forces. Unlike air and naval forces, ground forces require closer tactical cooperation in expeditionary

8

operations. As Dr. Thomas-Durell Young has correctly observed, "'(L)and forces' are not discrete independent units which can be easily employed tactically in combined operations (like ships and aircraft), but rather are comprised of combined arms teams made up of various subset formations, each of which may have different mission-essential tasks assigned to them."[16] As crisis response operations permit little time for mission preparation among coalition partners, mission success is jeopardized.

NATO's relatively recent adoption of multinational corps and multinational divisions is an attempt at greater integration but has fallen short primarily due to political sensibilities and the physical stationing of subordinate units in their parent countries rather than under the assigned headquarters. In his extensive studies on NATO's military structures, Young has identified three enduring major shortcomings with the multinational corps—command authority, transfer of authority, and corps CSS.[17] These deficiencies alone hamper effective deployment.

The issue of sovereignty has deprived multinational corps commanders of proper command authority. NATO allies balk at yielding crucial command authority to commanders of multinational corps in peacetime and insufficient command authority during non-Article 5 operations. Without the authority to train their subordinate units to standards in peacetime or the freedom to control them tactically during a conflict, corps commanders are hamstrung. By extension, the ambiguity concerning the "transfer of authority" (TOA), the moment when the contributing nation allows the commanding general to take charge of its forces, adds to the confusion.[18]

The opportunity for subordinate units composing multinational corps or multinational divisions to conduct collective training is limited because they are geographically separated by dozens of miles. Their first opportunity to operate together as a cohesive force is during

9

a deployment. Under such circumstances, operations in a crisis region will be sub par until units become accustomed to operating together. For crises that require decisive intervention, mission accomplishment will be endangered.

The absence of corps CSS units for all corps, except the Allied Command Europe Rapid Reaction Corps (ARRC), hamstrings rapid deployment of NATO land forces. Allied members do not even allocate CSS units to the multinational corps, and even earmarking such units in peacetime to specific corps remains unfulfilled. For any type of crisis response operation, CSS support becomes ad hoc, wasteful, and chaotic because the corps commanders will need to solicit contributions from respective nations during the deployment phase.[19] This state of affairs is hardly conducive to rapid decisive operations.

The Impact of Enduring Deficiencies on NATO Enlargement.

Whatever the problems associated with the old members contributing to the Alliance, they pale in comparison to the new members and the candidates' challenges. Simply put, assimilation into the Alliance is beyond the means of the newcomers in the short term unless NATO makes appropriate accommodations.

The New Members. Under NATO's current organizational structure, enlargement does little to strengthen the Alliance in real terms. Poland, Hungary, and the Czech Republic have added about 200,000 troops to the Alliance, but increased membership without the ability to harness the military potential provides more fat than muscle.[20]

In preparation for their inclusion in NATO's integrated military structure, Poland, Hungary, and the Czech Republic continue restructuring and modernizing their armed forces. Military reforms are progressing reasonably well but suffer from a lack of funding, and the pace of modernization is directly tied to economic progress and force reductions. If either falters, then so does the pace of modernization and reform.

Poland has undertaken a progressive restructuring and modernization program called the "Komorowski Plan," which is to culminate in 2006. The objective is to reduce its armed forces to 150,000 service members, of which 75,000 will be professional soldiers, by 2006. Conscription has been reduced to a 12-month service obligation. Poland is reducing the percentage of senior officers to 30 percent of the total force, and reorganizing its general staff along the lines of the U.S. Joint Staff. The army is buying 128 German Leopard 2A4 tanks, converting its T-72 tanks to NATO standards, producing a new infantry fighting vehicle (KTO), and making similar upgrades with other weapon systems. Of course, the pace of modernization greatly depends on the economy. Poland has declared four brigades for NATO's immediate and rapid reaction forces and two divisions for the main defense forces (30,000 troops total).[21]

Hungary's 10-year modernization plan comprises three phases ending in 2010. Hungary is reducing its armed forces to 37,500 by 2003 and plans to end conscription by 2010. It is reorganizing the general staff along the lines of the U.S. Joint Staff. It has declared a combat battalion, a military intelligence company, two antiaircraft platoons, and military police unit for the Immediate Reaction Force, a brigade to the ARRC, and one tank brigade, five infantry brigades, as well as antiaircraft, artillery, engineer and support units for the main defense forces. Hungary has provided the Tászár Air Base in support of the Bosnia peace mission, and Hungary's geographic location provides NATO with access to the Balkans.[22]

The Czech Republic has no formal plans to reduce the armed forces, but a general staff study recommends a reduction to 45,000 by 2010. It is retaining conscription with a 12-month service obligation. The army is upgrading around 120 of its T-72 tanks and plans to modernize 70 percent of its equipment. Additionally, the air force is investing in a modern L-159 subsonic fighter jet. The Czech Republic has allotted 8,400 troops for the immediate and rapid reaction forces and has declared its rapid reaction brigade to the ARRC by 2002 (47,000 troops total).[23]

The fact remains that the new NATO members are having trouble integrating into the Alliance. The Soviet military doctrinal legacy persists. All have hundreds of T-55 tanks, which are obsolete. Poland's armed forces still have a low level of training. Most training is conducted at battalion level and only in garrison instead of the field. Brigade level exercises are infrequent. Pilots only fly 60 hours per year, whereas the NATO minimum standard is 120 hours. The Hungarian army conducts inadequate training, is not "modern" (e.g., lacking unit tasks, conditions, and standards), and has too much obsolete Soviet equipment. Defense spending has recently declined to 1.51 percent due to the diversion of funds for natural disaster relief. Initial force reductions disproportionately affected the manpower levels of operational units, resulting in a manpower deficit. The Czech army conducts no training above company level and needs to improve its English language training. Most of its equipment is also of obsolete Soviet make. The L-159 fighter jet is consuming 70 percent of the military budget and does not seem worth the investment since its pilot training averages 60 hours per year.[24]

Attempting to reach technical interoperability is an expensive process and in view of the old members' difficulties in attaining the DCI objectives, the prognosis for new members with their nascent market economies is that technical interoperability problems will persist. Procedural interoperability is a matter of training with NATO procedures. Given the Soviet military doctrinal legacy and the infrequent opportunities to train with other NATO partners, internalizing NATO procedures will likely proceed slowly.

The Candidate States. The members of NATO's Membership Action Plan (MAP): Estonia, Latvia, Lithuania, Bulgaria, Romania, Slovenia, Slovak Republic, Albania, and the Former Yugoslavian Republic of Macedonia, are candidates for membership during the Prague Summit in November 2002. While some have a better chance than others this round, all suffer from persistent military capability problems.

As with NATO members, the NATO candidates must contribute 2 percent of their GDP to defense spending. At first glance, NATO's requirement may seem arbitrary since so many NATO members do not meet the requirement, but the 2 percent apportionment goal ensures candidates devote sufficient funding to the military for the transition into NATO's integrated military structure. Currently, only Bulgaria, Macedonia, and Romania can meet the standard (Table 2).

State	Active Force Size, 2000[a]	Defense Expenditures, (FY)[b]	Percent GDP Military Expenditure, (FY)[b]	Defense Expenditure per Troop in US $[c]
MAP States				
Albania	47,000	$ 42 million (99)	1.5 (99)	$894
Bulgaria	79,760	$344 million (00)	2.4 (00)	$4,313
Estonia	4,800	$70 million (99)	1.2 (99)	$14,583
Latvia	5,050	$60 million (99)	0.9(99)	$11,881
Lithuania	12,700	$181 million (99)	1.7 (99)	$14,252
Macedonia	16,000	$76.3 million (00)	2.2 (00)	$4,769
Romania	207,000	$720 million (00)	2.2 (00)	$3,478
Slovakia	38,600	$380 million (00)	1.7 (00)	$9,844
Slovenia	9,000	$370 million (00)	1.7 (00)	$41,111

[a] IISS, *The Military Balance 2000-2001.*
[b] *CIA World Fact Book.*
[c] Derived by dividing Defense Expenditures by Active Force Size.

Table 2. Defense Expenditures.

Defense expenditures per troop, depicting the general sophistication of the armed forces, are much more problematic. The NATO European median is $82,602 (Italy), with Poland having the lowest expenditure of $14,727. A low figure of defense expenditures per troop indicates a lower level of technological sophistication, making interoperability very difficult to attain. Taken together, these figures determine whether a candidate nation is a potential contributor or a parasite to NATO.[25] Only Estonia, Lithuania, Slovakia, and Slovenia meet or surpass Poland. No candidate shows much promise of attaining interoperability without significant assistance.

An overview of candidate armed forces reveals that persistent, deep-rooted problems will mar any contributions to NATO's integrated military structure. Enlargement does enhance stability and increase European security, but in the realm of military capabilities, NATO's military structure will not benefit much.

Albania's active army consists of 40,000 soldiers, of which 22,500 are conscripts (12-month service obligation). The active force structure is in the process of reform and should comprise seven divisions and a commando brigade. The navy has 2,500 sailors operating numerous coast guard vessels. The air force has 4,500 airmen operating 98 combat aircraft; of course, how many are actually operational is questionable. The equipment is a mixture of old Soviet and Chinese origin.[26] Interoperability with NATO would be poor.

The Bulgarian army has an active force of 42,400, of which 33,300 are conscripts (12-month service obligation). The active force structure consists of four mechanized infantry divisions, four armor brigades, three mechanized infantry brigades, one airborne brigade, and several air defense and artillery regiments. The navy has 5,260 sailors (2,000 conscripts) with one submarine, a frigate, and several coast guard vessels. The air force has 18,300 airmen with 181 combat aircraft and 43 attack helicopters. Pilots average 30 to 40 flying hours per year. All equipment is Soviet vintage, much of it quite old.[27] Interoperability with NATO would be poor.

Estonia's active army consists of 4,800 soldiers, of which 2,870 are conscripts (12-month service obligation). The active force structure comprises five infantry battalions, one artillery battalion, one guard battalion, and one reconnaissance battalion. The navy has 250 sailors (140 conscripts) with several coast guard vessels. The air force has 140 airmen operating 3 aircraft and 7 helicopters. Pilot training averages 70 flying hours per year. Equipment is scant and of Soviet origin.[28] Interoperability with NATO would be poor.

The Latvian active army has 2,400 soldiers, including 1,690 conscripts (12-month service obligation). The active force structure consists of one infantry battalion, one reconnaissance battalion, one Special Forces team, one peacekeeping company, and one artillery unit. The navy has 840 sailors (360 conscripts) with several coast guard vessels. The air force has 210 airmen operating 19 aircraft and 4 helicopters.[29] Equipment is of Soviet origin and old, and interoperability with NATO would be poor.

Lithuania's active army has 9,340 soldiers, including 3,720 conscripts (12-month service obligation). The active force structure comprises two motorized rifle brigades, one light infantry battalion, one engineer battalion, and one peacekeeping company. The navy has 560 sailors (280 conscripts) manning several coast guard vessels. The air force has 800 airmen operating 27 aircraft and 12 helicopters.[30] Equipment is of Soviet origin and old. Interoperability with NATO would be poor.

Macedonia has an active force of 16,000 soldiers, of which 8,000 are conscripts (9-month service obligation). The active force structure consists of 2 brigades and a border guard brigade. The air force has 700 airmen operating 10 aircraft and 4 helicopters. The equipment is a mixture of quite old Soviet origin and U.S. equipment.[31] Interoperability with NATO would be poor.

The Romanian active army has 106,000 active soldiers, including 71,000 conscripts (12-month service obligation). The active force structure has about 18 mechanized infantry brigades, 7 armor brigades, 7 mountain brigades, 1 guards brigade, 1 engineer regiment, and several air defense and artillery brigades. The navy comprises 20,800 (12,600 conscripts) with 1 submarine, 1 destroyer, 6 frigates, and several coast guard vessels. Moreover, it has 10,200 marine infantry. The air force has 43,500 airmen (25,000 conscripts). It possesses 323 combat aircraft and 16 attack helicopters with pilots having an average of 40 flying hours per year. Two airborne brigades also belong to the air force. Much of the equipment is Soviet made and very old. [32] Interoperability with NATO would be poor.

Slovakia has an active army of 23,800 soldiers, of which 13,600 are conscripts (12-month service obligation). The active force structure has an armor brigade, a mechanized infantry brigade, an artillery brigade, and a rapid reaction battalion. The air force comprises 11,500 airmen with 84 combat aircraft and 19 attack helicopters. Pilot training averages 45 flying hours per year. All the equipment is Soviet vintage and would have poor interoperability with NATO.[33]

Slovenia's active army contains 9,000 soldiers, of which 4,000 to 5,000 are conscripts (7-month service obligation). The active force structure comprises seven infantry battalions, two independent mechanized battalions, one Special Forces brigade, a surface-to-air missile brigade, an aviation brigade (eight armed helicopters), and an artillery battalion. All equipment is a mixture of Soviet and Yugoslavian production and would have poor interoperability with NATO.[34]

Conscription makes up 50 percent or more of the candidate nation armed forces. The retention of conscription is likely to remain in the near term because of the expense associated with professional armies. Depending on the laws regarding the deployment of conscripts, the actual size of a deploying force for crisis response may be a mere pittance.

The size of the armed forces, especially for Article 5 missions, is a serious issue regarding integration into a battle. For high tempo combat operations, force size contributions below a brigade are of dubious value since they are difficult to integrate into larger maneuver units capable of conducting combat tasks. A national contribution of a combat battalion or company would need to be integrated into a brigade or division in order to generate the needed combat power for successful combat operations. If such small units have no opportunity to conduct extensive, collective training with their host brigades prior to a military operation, they will lack the necessary skills to accomplish assigned missions. Since a contribution of a brigade-sized force is beyond the capabilities of smaller members, NATO must address how to integrate smaller combat units into its structure.

Countries with Soviet equipment, especially aircraft, would have severe difficulties operating with NATO. Differences in communications, avionics, and computerization would hamper interoperability. Soviet-made aircraft would not participate in a NATO air campaign because of incompatibilities and the dangers of fratricide. Soviet armored vehicles, particularly the older models, would create more confusion that contribution. The inventories of all the MAP countries consist of Soviet T55 and T72 tanks as well as BTR and BMP armored personnel carriers, which either need to be scrapped or upgraded to NATO standards. Upgrading Soviet vehicles to NATO standards may create fresh problems, given the plethora of Soviet exports during the Cold War to potential adversaries. Given the fog of war in conflicts, NATO members would have problems distinguishing friend from foe and risk fratricide. In the final analysis, it is cheaper and easier simply to invest in western equipment and weapons.

The Necessary Restructuring.

Clearly, the European contribution to NATO is deteriorating. Without an imminent threat, NATO's European partners are unlikely to devote a greater part of their GDP to defense. Because power projection is a stated task of crisis management missions and because the European allies are unwilling or unable to improve these capabilities, NATO must make some innovative reforms. Otherwise, the United States will continue to bear the lion's share of every conflict and operation.

The Integrated Multinational Division and the Impact on New Members. The Alliance must adopt a force structure that allows the assimilation of new members into the integrated military structure. The Cold War approach of separate national divisions within the Alliance was sufficient under pure collective defense, but, with the addition of collective security tasks, interoperability and defense budget austerity assume greater prominence.

The Alliance needs to take the bold step and transform its divisions into IMDs. Such an initiative allows the member states to downsize their aggregate force contribution without reducing their commitment to the Alliance. Additionally, such divisions permit assured and swift integration and interoperability of new members.

The IMD reconciles the deficiencies associated with multinational units. As Thomas-Durell Young correctly points out, "multinational land formations are, by their very nature, less efficient and **less effective** than a similar pure national formation. Differences in language, weapon systems, organization, logistics, and procedures, all hinder the operation of multinational formations."[35] Such friction occurs because multinational units rarely operate as an integrated force until thrown together for a crisis. The IMD model mitigates this friction by integrating allies at a much lower level and co-locating all the division subordinate units.

As a matter of illustration, transforming a U.S. division into an IMD is a relatively easy process. Retaining its divisional headquarters, a maneuver brigade, and an aviation brigade, the U.S. IMD allocates unit assignments according to new members' contributive capabilities and size (Figure 1). In this manner, new members can specialize, that is, modernize selected units instead of attempting to modernize their entire armed forces immediately. Because smaller countries can only contribute small forces (ranging in size from a company to brigade), these units would make a greater contribution as an integral part of a division. Integrating smaller units into an IMD is much more manageable than clustering a multinational corps with dozens of discrete, small units. Each unit retains its existing organizational structure since its soldiers are accustomed to it, and it is unlikely to have a negative impact on military operations. Contributing members retain their national integrity through their units and are responsible for personnel and equipment requirements. Participating nations would also contribute personnel to the division headquarters, combat support, and combat service support units.

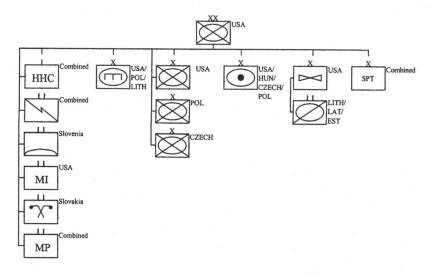

Figure 1. Idealized Integrated Multination Division.

19

The question of sovereignty is a crucial issue. No nation likes the idea of another country commanding its forces. "Nations have been loath to give up command authorities over land forces to foreign commanders out of fear that, *inter alia*, they will be 'fragmented' or improperly commanded."[36] Given the size of each unit contribution, fragmentation is not an issue. The issue of command authority is a matter of trust, which resolves itself after a period of training and familiarization with the division. In matters of training, the unit commander retains full responsibility. Naturally, he submits his training plan to division for final review and approval, but this administrative function does not impinge on his own command authority. For contributing members the advantages are self-evident—yielding a modicum of sovereignty in exchange for assured contributions to the Alliance.

The IMD provides the opportunity for all members to demonstrate their value to the Alliance. It may seem a small matter, but competitive activities, such as tank and artillery gunnery, marksmanship matches, and Best Ranger competition, as well as the participation in the Expert Infantryman Badge and Expert Medical Badge tests, greatly enhance individual and unit pride and *esprit de corps*. Working towards tangible goals and being rewarded for them probably do more to engender NATO cohesion than any other factor. The IMD is the best vehicle for building this sense of belongingness.

To improve equipment interoperability, NATO allies may lease or sell equipment to new members. Such an approach to integration is much cheaper than expecting new members to develop and produce needed equipment on their own. For its own IMD, the United States can offer to lease or sell existing division organic equipment that is already in Europe. Regardless, each contributing member state can focus its modernization to key units initially and modernize the rest of its armed forces over time. If the contributor accepts the U.S. sell/lease program, the supply channels are strictly American. If not, the supply channels emanate from the contributing country. Each member state assigns maintenance and supply troops to the combat service support brigade. In this manner, member countries become accustomed to U.S. maintenance, supply, and reporting procedures. The same approach holds true for the rest of the Alliance.

To improve procedural interoperability, participation in training activities, such as weapons qualification, individual and collective training, field exercises, and planning processes, expose new members to NATO's military methods and procedures, enhancing the integration process immensely. The new NATO members are not thoroughly familiar with the concepts of Task, Conditions, and Standards, the Mission Essential Task Listing, Troop Leading Procedures, the five-paragraph Operations Order, the Deliberate Decision-Making Process, and so forth. Most of these concepts require some mentoring because they are Western in design and a little arcane, particularly for the military cultures steeped in Soviet doctrine. Relying solely on classroom instruction to teach NATO-compatible procedures and practices is not sufficient because the concepts require frequent application in training. Without practice and personal assistance, new members may give up in frustration and simply go through the motions. Under the tutelage of their NATO hosts, they can focus on these concepts and procedures, resolve issues as they arise, and assimilate them.

One of the greatest obstacles for the armed forces of new members is learning English. Language immersion is the most effective and quickest way for non-English speakers to gain proficiency. Use of existing host nation facilities, barracks, and housing, as well as access to television and radio programs (British Broad Cast, Armed Forces Network, etc.), would expose foreign national soldiers and their families to English and Western culture. Daily contacts with host nation soldiers and families also expose new members to Western democratic values. Since the NATO Security Investment Program (NSIP) pays for the infrastructure, opening existing casernes to new members would actually lower expenses. Immediate use of existing barracks, training areas, ranges, housing, and facilities provide powerful incentives for new member states. It is highly unlikely that any country would pass up such an opportunity. Furthermore, the influence of the Western armed forces will slowly permeate the contributing nations as soldiers rotate through the IMD.

Admittedly, some cultural differences merit mention. For instance, some contributing nations may permit female soldiers in combat units or gays in the military. Such issues remain within the purview of the relevant commander, and the host nation headquarters should accommodate the cultural differences without derailing the integrated concept.

The IMDs permit greater participation in collective defense and the new crisis response missions. Integrated membership negates the ad hoc character of contingency missions and allows all members, regardless of their size, to participate more effectively and efficiently. In this manner, instead of the few shouldering the burden of security, responsibility is evenly distributed throughout the Alliance.

Although the initial readiness of the IMD will be low, readiness will increase rapidly with the series of phased, train-up activities, culminating in certification. As with any initiative, the devil is in the details, but the U.S. Army can meet these challenges and truly integrate new members into the Alliance. Once this initiative is proven, other NATO countries can elect to adopt the IMD structure with new and old members, producing thoroughly modern and cohesive units at less cost and manpower.

The Impact on the Rest of the Alliance. The IMD could provide crucial opportunities for all Alliance members. Given the inadequate military spending expenditures, manpower and technology deficiencies, and lowered readiness, the IMD could permit allies to consolidate their scarce military resources. Countries could equip their designated IMD units with the most modern and lighter equipment and weapon systems and fill the ranks with professional soldiers vice conscripts. NATO's Defense Requirements Review, which determines the number of divisions based on mission needs, will need to adjust the numbers if the IMD concept is adopted.

The ARRC already has a number of standard, multinational divisions, so the framework for a transition to the IMD exists. The 10 divisions of the ARRC are sufficient to conduct crisis management and immediate collective defense. The ARRC would comprise high readiness land forces, meaning they receive priority in manpower, funding, and modernization. To be truly effective though, the subordinate units of each IMD must be physically consolidated under a designated headquarters. The host country, with funding from the NSIP, would be responsible for implementing the infrastructure upgrades for air and sea ports of debarkation. The existing national headquarters should remain in order to minimize turmoil. Multinational Division (South) remains unspecified, but France is well-positioned to stand it up if it is so disposed, and the facilities in southern France are sufficient to support it. The U.S. 173d Airborne Brigade in Vicenza, Italy is logically positioned fill out the 3d Italian Infantry Division (Mechanized) (Table 3).[37]

A U.S. Interim Brigade Combat Team (IBCT) can comprise the immediate reaction force of the ARRC, permitting rapid deployment of the most modern force and underscoring America's continued commitment to the Alliance. Its stationing near Ramstein Air Base in Germany (perhaps nearby Baumholder) ensures rapid deployment.

Division Headquarters	IMD Location
ARRC Headquarters	Mönchengladbach, Germany
1st U.S. Armor Division	Bad Kreuznach, Germany
7th GE Armor Division	Düsseldorf, Germany
2d GR Infantry Division (Mechanized)	Edhessa, Greece
1st TU Infantry Division (Mechanized)	Turkey
SP Rapid Reaction Division	Madrid, Spain
3d UK Infantry Division (Mechanized): framework division with Italian brigade component	Bulford, England
1st UK Armor Division with Danish component	Herford, Germany
3d IT Infantry Division (Mechanized): framework division with Portuguese brigade component	Milan, Italy
Multinational Division (Central): BE/NL/GE/UK	Mönchengladbach, Germany (slated for elimination, but the author recommends its retention)
Multinational Division (South)	France (author's recommendation)

Table 3. ARRC Integrated Multinational Divisions.

The ARRC needs a Special Forces Group (SFG) comprising teams from all Alliance members in order to ensure early engagement into potential crisis regions. The amount of expertise and knowledge that the various member states' special forces possess makes the ARRC SFG indispensable. The former U.S. Special Forces caserne at Bad Tolz, Germany, would be a perfect location for training.

The ARRC has an established CSS capability (actually the only NATO corps CSS), which all members can augment without effort or added expense.[38] Given his unique position, the ARRC commander would need an "Integrated Directing and Control Authority" similar to the authority granted to the commanding general of the I German/Netherlands Corps. This authority is needed to assure that the forces are trained according to task, conditions, and standards. Upon alert, the TOA automatically falls to the ARRC commander in order to permit proper command and control.[39] The command of the ARRC rotates among the allies, demonstrating not only shared contributions but also shared authority. In this matter, all the Allies have a chance to be chiefs instead of indians.

Streamlining NATO's Subordinate Corps. The divisions of the lower readiness forces operate with reduced readiness without a significant impact on the effectiveness of the Alliance. Other than mobilization for a major war, activation of the lower readiness forces is predicated on the augmentation or rotation of deployed ARRC divisions in a crisis region. Pragmatically, establishing higher and lower readiness forces permits the European allies to focus assets on their designated IMD units. The economic savings in essential areas—lower manpower requirements, fewer units to maintain, and fewer weapons and equipment to field—permit a greater focus on technological innovations. Although fewer divisions represent a calculated risk, the smaller, integrated ARRC permits the Europeans to resolve the DCI deficiencies at less cost, manpower, and resources.

Despite the reliance on the ARRC for most missions, the Alliance will still need to maintain at least two additional corps headquarters (EUROCORPS and EUROFOR) for extended peace support operations. These additional command and control headquarters are crucial to ensure key corps staff, communications, and intelligence personnel, among others, are not overdeployed. Sustaining a peace support operation requires that personnel and equipment have a chance to recover; otherwise the system begins to break down. These headquarters require the most modern and robust command and control systems in order to communicate to the parent headquarters and host nations, as well as the forward deployed subordinate units. Command and control cannot be an ad hoc affair with obsolete systems.

Conclusion.

Establishing IMDs allows faster assimilation of new members as well as increasing interoperability within NATO. The opportunity to buy or lease western equipment allows new members to invest more money into their economies, which is an important goal for emerging market economies. Designating a few units for the IMD allows new countries to specialize and modernize without exorbitant defense budgets. Integration precludes the need of individual nations establishing separate logistical units in support of contingency missions. New members will acquire greater proficiency of English through immersion. By frequent participation in collective training, new members gain a greater appreciation for NATO training, planning, maintenance, and supply procedures. Moreover, soldiers and their families gain a greater understanding of Western democratic values and culture, which in turn will find its way to the home country, forging greater bonds.

If the Alliance does not adopt the IMD concept, NATO will not realize its full potential as a cohesive force. Enlargement will add to the collection of members, but the contributions of individual members will be limited. Heretofore, the burden of military operations rested on a few members. The current structure does not allow all members to contribute to every operation because the Alliance cannot integrate them fully. The IMD paradigm allows integration of even the smallest members and permits greater economy in military spending. Under this structure, members may be able to lower their military spending to 1.5 percent of their GDP without a drop in capabilities.

Recommendations.

The United States can improve its strategic position and cohesion by pursuing the following:

- Convert the two U.S. divisions in Europe into IMDs in order to assist in the assimilation of new members into the Alliance.

- Encourage other NATO members to adopt this model in order to make more effective use of their military spending and resources.

- Establish the ARRC as NATO's higher readiness force for all missions and maintain the EUROCORPS and EUROFOR corps headquarters, sufficiently staffed and equipped with the most modern and robust command and control systems. Rotate the command of the ARRC among the contributing members.

- Expand the existing ARRC CS and CSS base into an Area Support Group (ASG) equivalent to provide assured logistics during training and deployments. The ASG must be sufficiently large to support multiple rotations during extended PSO.

NATO cannot afford to rest on its laurels and transform the Alliance into a European country club. NATO embodies U.S. European policy at 30 percent of the cost to the United States. The Alliance provides hope to nonmembers and security for members. The restructuring to IMDs ensures that NATO remains relevant, resolves many of the current command authority and training issues and eliminates the need for superfluous and potentially competing European military security initiatives. The emerging strategic environment demands greater efficiency and cooperation among the Alliance members, and the integrated multinational division structure meets these challenges.

ENDNOTES

1. Dr. Andrew Dorman, *European Adaptation to Expeditionary Warfare: Implications for the United States Army*, Washington: Joint Services Command and Staff College, Defense Studies Department, publication pending, p. 8.

2. Thomas S. Szayna, "NATO Enlargement: Forecasting the 'Who' and 'When'," *National Security Studies Quarterly*, Summer 2001, Vol. VII, Issue 3, p. 44. Hereafter referred to as Szayna, "Forecasting."

3. John J. Lis and Zachary Selden, *Integrating New Allies Into NATO*, Washington: Congressional Budget Office, Internet *http://www.cbo.gov*, Chapter 2, p. 1. Hereafter referred to as Lis, *Integrating*. John J. Lis and Zachary Selden, *NATO Burdensharing After Enlargement*, Washington: Congressional Budget Office, August 2001, Internet, *http://www.cbo.gov/showdoc.cfm?index-2976& sequence=0&from=0*, Chapter 1, p. 14. Hereafter referred to as Lis, *Burdensharing*. Hungary is projected to increase its expenditure to 1.8 percent by 2001.

4. Szayna, *Forecasting*, pp. 44-45. Lis, *Integrating*, chapter 2, p. 1.

5. Loren Thompson, "New Century, Old Question: Can Europe Keep Up?" *Sea Power Magazine*, January 2000, Internet, *http://www. lexingtoninstitiute.org/defense/newcent.htm*, pp. 4-5. John G. McGinn and Timothy Liston, "Beyond the Rhetoric and Acronyms: The Reality of European Military Capabilities," *National Security Studies Quarterly*, Vol. VII, Issue 1, Winter 2001, pp. 78, 82-83.

6. Dorman, p. 8.

7. McGinn, p. 87; Dorman, pp. 10-11.

8. *Ibid*, p. 92.

9. *Defense Capabilities Initiative*, NATO Press Release, April 25, 1999, Internet, *http://www.nato.int/docu/pr/1999/p99s069e.htm*, p. 1.

10. *Driving Capability Transformations*, SACLANT/NATO Themes 2000, Internet, *http://www.saclant.nato.int/pio/FACTS/ themes00.htm*, p. 11. Hereafter referred to as *Transformations*.

11. *Ibid*, p. 11. The salient shortfalls are as follows:

• Deployable support units and capabilities for land, maritime, and air forces;

• Maritime communications systems;

• Guaranteed availability of strategic sea and airlift for rapid deployment of forces, particularly for non-Article 5 operations; and,

• Specialized capabilities such as air-to-air refueling, tankers, surveillance and reconnaissance assets, Theater Ballistic Missile Defense, NBC protection and protection capabilities.

12. *The Alliance's Strategic Concept*, April 24, 1999, Internet, *http://www.nato.int/docu/pr/1999/p99-065e.htm*, paras. 10 and 12. Hereafter referred to as *Concept*.

13. John J. Lis and Zachary Selden, *NATO Burdensharing After Enlargement*, Washington: Congressional Budget Office, August 2001, Internet, *http://www.cbo.gov/showdoc.cfm?index-2976& sequence=0&from=0*, Chapter 1, p. 7. McGinn, pp. 84-85. Dorman, p. 9. The United Kingdom, Netherlands, France, and Belgium have professional armies; Germany, Italy, and Spain have partial conscription; Sweden and Norway have retained conscription.

14. USNI military database, Internet, *http://www.periscope. ucg.com/nations/nato/index.html*. Portugal's conscription ranges from 4 to 8 months in the army and 4 to 18 months in the other services. Germany has opted for partial conscription, meaning that citizens serve for 9 months as conscripts and then receive the increased benefits of a volunteer army if they decide to remain. Germany permits a limited number of conscripts to volunteer to extend their service to 23 months in order to participate in peace support operations.

15. Thomas-Durell Young, *Multinational Land Formations and NATO: Reforming Practices and Structures*, Carlisle Barracks: U.S. Army War College, Strategic Studies Institute, December 1997, p. 7. Hereafter referred to as Young, *MLF and NATO*.

16. Thomas-Durell Young, *Reforming NATO's Military Structures: The Long-Term Study and Its Implications for Land Forces*, Carlisle Barracks: U.S. Army War College, Strategic Studies Institute, May 15, 1998, p. 18. Hereafter referred to as Young, *Reforming NATO*.

17. Young, *MLF and NATO*; Young, *Reforming NATO*; Thomas-Durell Young, *Multinational Land Forces and the NATO Force Structure Review*, Carlisle Barracks: U.S. Army War College: Strategic Studies Institute, June 2000. Hereafter referred to as Young, *MLF and NATO Force Structure*.

18. Young, *MLF and NATO Force Structure*, pp. 6-9, 11-12; Young, *MLF and NATO*, pp. 13-14.

19. Young, *MLF and NATO Force Structure*, p. 10.

20. Department of State, *The Enlargement of NATO: Why Adding Poland, Hungary, and the Czech Republic to NATO Strengthens American National Security*, Washington: U.S. Department of State, 1998, p. 14.

21. Lis, *Integrating*, Summary, p. 3, Chapter 3, pp. 1-2; Wojciech Luczak, "Polish Land Forces Trimming into 21st Century," *Military Technology*, Vol. 25, Issue 8, August 2001, pp. 98-103; Anonymous, "The Polish Armed Force Restructuring and Modernization Plan (2001-2006)," *NATO's Nations and Partners for Peace*, Monch Media, Inc, 2001, pp. 152-153.

22. Lis, *Integrating*, Summary, p. 4, Chapter 2, p. 4, Chapter 3, pp. 2-3 and 8; Laszlo Szabo and Gyula Bene, "On the Way to a Modern Force: The Restructuring Program of the Hungarian Defense Forces," *NATO's Nations and Partners for Peace*, Monch Media, Inc, 2001, pp. 148-150; Hungary; Internet *http://www.periscope.ucg.com/nations/nato/hungary/index.html*.

23. Lis, *Integrating*, Summary, p. 4, Chapter 3, pp. 3-4; Jeffrey Ulbrich, "Czech Military a Long March From Being a Full Contributor to NATO," *The Los Angeles Times*, February 25, 2001, p. A8.

24. Lis, *Integrating*, Chapter 1, pp. 2-3, Chapter 3, pp. 1-4; Ulbrich, p. A8; Szabo and Bene, p. 149.

25. Szayna, *Forecasting*, pp. 44-45. The figures differ from Szayna's original calculations because he used older data files, but the conclusions remain valid.

26. *The Military Balance 2000-2001*, London: Oxford University Press, October 2000, p. 102. Hereafter referred to as *World Balance*; Internet *http://www.periscope.ucg.com/nations/nato/albania/index.html*.

27. *Ibid*, pp. 89-90.

28. *Ibid*, p. 93.

29. *Ibid*, p. 97.

30. *Ibid*, p. 98.

31. *Ibid*, pp. 98-99.

32. *Ibid*, pp. 100-101.

33. *Ibid*, p. 102.

34. *Ibid*, p. 102.

35. Young, *MLF and NATO Force Structure*, p. 9.

36. *Ibid.* (Emphasis in original.)

37. Young, *MLF and NATO*, pp 25-38 and 71-80. Dr. Young provides excellent details on NATO's multinational land formations, especially the ARRC.

38. *Ibid*, p. 72.

39. Thomas-Durell Young, "Multinational Land Forces and the NATO Force Structure Review," *RUSI Journal*, Vol. 145, Issue 4, August 2000, pp. 45-52. Dr. Young identifies lack of command authority and transfer of authority as crucial deficiencies within NATO. Additionally, the ARRC and MND(C) are the only multinational units with declared CSS formations. Hence, the ARRC is likely the best structure to integrate the IMD concept.